Uncoils a Snake

Also by Arthur J. Stewart

Rough Ascension and Other Poems of Science
Bushido: The Virtues of Rei and Makoto
Circle, Turtle, Ashes
The Ghost in the Word
From Where We Came
Elements of Chance
The Hallelujah Series and Other Poems

Uncoils a Snake

A POETRY CHAPBOOK

by Arthur J. Stewart

Periploi Press

NASHVILLE, TENNESSEE

2021

Design by Dariel Mayer
Periploi Presss / Nashville, TN

Manufactured in the United States of America

ISBN 978-0-9830115-9-0

For Monty

⁓

*who enjoys the koi pond
and Japanese maples,
just as I do.*

Contents

Preface and Acknowledgments

Archibald (Archie) Ammons (1926-2001) earned two National Books Awards, a National Book Critics Circle Award, the Library of Congress's Rebekah Johnson Bobbitt National Prize for Poetry, and the Bollingen Prize for Poetry [1]. His works have strongly influenced my own.

I first encountered Archie's poetry through *Glare* [2]. Upon reading *Glare* the first time, I was confused. Part One, titled Strip, consisted of 65 sections, each comprised of a variable number of stanzas; each stanza consisted of two lines. All of the lines were short, and the line breaks sometimes made sense and sometimes didn't. The meter was, if not absent, exceedingly rough and choppy. Punctuation was largely lacking, except for rare commas and an oddly large number of colons: the colons seemingly were used primarily as a substitute for periods. Occasionally, words were in all caps for emphasis; italicized words were used now and then, too, apparently for emphasis. Sentences, if that is what they were, were not separated by periods and did not start with a capital letter. And there was no shortage of "I"! What in *hell* was he *saying*? The meaning must be the important thing, I thought, because *Glare*'s structure—that is, the way it was built—seemed haphazard, almost to the point of slap-dash.

Glare, Part 2, titled Scat Scan, was more of the same. He skit-scatted from thought to thought, from observation to thought, from thought to observation. No fluff here, by golly! Terse, intelligent, whimsical, sometimes stretching deliberately for the absurd, and often reaching for the raw and rowdy, there it was: unbridled Archie to the world, plop, right here, right now. What should one do with it? How should one interpret it?

I took pause from *Glare* to review what is generally regarded as Ammons' finest poem, "Easter Morning." This poem, first published in *A Coast of Trees* [3], was stunningly beautiful, and I became an Ammons fan on the spot. I went back and reread *Glare*, from beginning to end, slower than before, and began to understand it; I began wallowing in it. Then, it was on to some of his other books—*A. R. Ammons Collected Poems, 1951-1971; A Coast of Trees; Garbage; The Selected Poems – Expanded Edition; Sphere*; and *Ommateum: With Doxology*. The list is long.

Later, I tried to emulate some of Archie's style: more colons, shorter lines, thought-carrying from stanza to stanza, observe-interpret, observe-interpret—the "I" is important here because the "I" is what interprets the observations. Poems that exclusively report observations often have less depth than those that include some perspective on human interpretation.

All of the poems in this collection were influenced strongly by Ammons' works, and for this I make no apology. Two poems in this collection, "How to Start the Thing Like Archie Did" and "I Lost It, Archie," have also been published in *The Hallelujah Series* [4]; another, "Transition to Summer" was previously published in *Elements of Chance* [5]. And as a special treat, Ammons' "Easter Morning," now in the public domain, is reprinted on pages 29-31 for your reading pleasure.

References

1. *www.poetryfoundation.org/poets/a-r-ammons*
2. Ammons, AR. 1997. *Glare*. W.W. Norton & Company, Inc. New York, NY.
3. Ammons, AR. 1981. *A Coast of Trees*. W.W. Norton & Company, Inc. New York, NY.
4. Stewart, AJ. 2021. *The Hallelujah Series and Other Poems*. Periploi Press, Nashville, TN.
5. Stewart, AJ. 2017. *Elements of Chance*. Celtic Cat Publishing, Knoxville, TN.

Uncoils a Snake

How to Start the Thing Like Archie Did

Doofus cat likes to nap
behind my computer's monitor and
she's black and she buries herself
on the desk in shadow: settles down

promptly unlike me and
starts snoring. Sometimes she scratches
her jowls on the corner of the monitor,
forcing it

off-kilter: cat-er-wampus. So many things
disrupt flow, add burbles, curlicues, off-
center adjustments of mass or velocity,
ovoids

rather than spheres, off-sets, things bend
toward lower energy: how much
is the question –
bending, I mean: should one genuflect

on one knee or on two, or go prone
with rump up, or flat out, in
maximum state of appeasement? Toes,
knees, belly and chin to ground

if that might help
although I know of no
righteous reason why it might be so, so unless
the party to be appeased appreciates

proneness in particular: perhaps
that position is
less threatening as it is
used by other animals expressing sub-

servience to their ilk: roll over, go
belly-up and ex-
pose the throat. And then just spring
from ilk to elk or silk or milk, it's

a piece of rhubarb pie or cake:

LET'ER RIP

Archie Does It Again

Near the end
of June, humidity

creeping up: I can't get enough
of *Glare*: turn pages

like slabs, cracks show, sure,
granite does that too

with time, but the strips
slither, scrape, bend, penetrate, come out

crusty but alive—he did it
again and again, creating

a mud-man of the self
from mundane stuff: health, thoughts,

the human condition.

Chickens et cetera

1.

It seems like this: once I fed a batch of left-
over spaghetti to the chickens: our shining

black ones, the ones that wandered
together like queens in a loose flock

out back, bug-hunting in the tall grass:
that day they ran like hell

to the spaghetti pile fast, their necks stretched
out, their wings half-spread

to get to the goodies quick, maybe thinking
in their little heads, behind orange eyes,

albino worms, or long maggots. Yum!
Those strands got swallowed quick

as a snake. That's the kind of thing to talk about:
a curling want with muscle to it—something

cold and pale can still be OK, but then
it should be matched

with something wiggling:
dark: warm: alive.

2.

Item two: the door is shut
tight enough to squeak. I'm exhausted

from trying to write, and from not
enough sleep. Now, there's a thing: last night

I did sleep some and dreamed: looking
into a man-made pool I saw fish—

one pale and huge, a meter long—I dashed
a big dip-net down to catch the thing

but did not succeed: it swam
lazily out of reach. I think

my life swims lazily out of reach.
But you know it's hard to tell.

3.

Archie notes a fault
that can't be mended is not a fault

at all: thick stuff
to think about, on a good day, this—

so of course I had to step outside
to think. And since there's not a northward

breeze (the air is solid still) I hear
18-wheeler trucks: their never-ending move

on US 40 east and west at night a mile
or two away—it seems a sacrilege:

and dogs: two big ones from the sound—
thank god they're far-off: they've lost

any sense of propriety they may have had
genetically: and their breeders too,

flooding us with useless mutts: splayed hips,
or spots, or hair or not or long ears or not and

even the tendency to drool. Can you imagine
designing a poodle? What fool

engineer would sign his name to that? I note
katydids that saw the dusk and early dark

do not
stridulate near dawn: wiser

Ode to *Glare*

1.

Two mid-day hours
of mower-riding spent

to send the upper half of the grass to hell
is hell in June—the humidity alone

is enough to hurt and the glare
and the diversity of bugs

small as gnats that stick
to the sweaty neck and cheek—

I'm glad
at least they avoid the eyes

but the ears
they seem to like as well.

2.

What the heck is he doing
a reader has the right to ask

and how does that
pertain to me? If that's

the central issue the issue is
too central, that's

for sure. Stand back
shade the eyes to knock off glare.

3.

A solid sphere of glass
can focus the light and burn

a table upon which it sits.
strip

off the wax, the cherry stain—
whatever it takes: the job's

simple in concept: bring it, buster,
to the grain

Transition to Summer

In *Glare*, Archie shined
his copper pots and pans: he hung
words out there, stubby rafts
crafted in gnarly hood-winked lines.
So what are we to make of such?
For one, they ready me to fire up and off, like a

bottle-rocket this sudden time of year—
just scratch the match and touch it

to the fuse: this is,
        after all,
just a warm-up, a prelude to the blander
blue blanket of summer: lay it
on the new-mown grass; the fire-

flies are hanging around, total dead-
beats in terms of large movements
but beating their little wings
like mad in the cooling air and

out there, in the neighborhood,
someone is grilling: the char-
coal-blasted de-
licious odor of burgers
makes me want a beer.

How Archie Did It

Sometimes he just rambled
for lines and lines, not saying much

until out of the blue, bang
he uncoils

a snake, steps back, looks
it over: diamonds, or mottled

like a copperhead or lean
as a racer, no need to poke

the thing with a stick, it's there
and that's enough—see, no eyelids, no

external ears, count
the number of scales between the eyes

Back to Archie

I discover a
need to go back
to Archie—he was so clear
and full of lively mud

this thing for example
shoots out there and that thing
goes the other way and
who knows about item three: it could be

and the two dogs
after their breakfast
this morning took some time outdoors then
came in and got busy de-

stuffing their chew-toys
the fluffs
of artificial cotton look like snow
puffs, here, there

and the toy skunk grows thin
outside it is chill but OK: buds
on the dogwood are swelling
hard, the Yoshino cherry is

getting ready to break free
the surface of the soil warms
under the sun: the daffodils
of course don't care

From Archie to Japan and Almost Back

He threaded his stuff on a strip
page after page, wish I

could do a thing like that and
off again, it's not over yet, things

will change: the sea-
floor earthquake that ripped Japan

several days ago was a big'un, initiating
tsunamis—more than one

technically speaking with the whole Earth
ringing like a bell

and if you were there probably
you, too, ringing like a bell but

just slippage, at its roots. We should know
better by now, she'll have her way and he

showed how he couldn't
go straight down the road

and there
you have it: the reactor

fizzing sea-water, and sea-water
having smashed what it could now oozing

downhill back home, bricks
tumbling or sliding still

from where they were to new
locations of temporary

stability with aftershocks

A Short Ode to Archie

The Archie Ammons guy who was
is dead: but his books
remain
like cement nails

pounded in the head.
I wish I'd met him
eye to eye and thought to thought—
like Cat-in-the-Hat:

I think I'd like him quite a lot.

Japanese Ornamental Maple

Archie said the purpose of living
is being alive.
And perhaps that's true, but
perhaps there's no purpose

except that of being
a dissipater of energy: a thing that converts
energetic states to lower-energy states—
that is, entropy generation, fulfilling

in part the overwhelming
physical need of the
universe. Bit players
with big thoughts, high hopes,

wonderful dreams. On the lawn
this morning a few more yellow leaves from the
elm and the tulip poplar trees—both tree-types
have become burned out by summer,

and there, beneath the large red maple, the papery
remains of the bald-faced hornets' nest
taken down several days ago by the
bold pest-control technician. I wish

I had been there to see it: did he
dance a bit or hold steady as the
pesticide stream ruptured the gray-paper
walls and soaked the chunky black bodies, as the

pallid white larvae and pupae spilled
to the grass like little white beans? Their dreams
are gone. That evening the wife and I sat
in lawn chairs at the entrance to the garage:

looked out
at a few more yellow leaves and at the carnage left
on the lawn, and particularly at one limb
on a near-by Japanese ornamental maple that

went off at an odd angle
fulfilling its want despite
the tidy pathways of other limbs on the same tree and
we considered and discussed: should we

lop it off, fulfilling our desire to make
the tree look balanced, or should we
allow it to have its willful way? Righteously,
which will should prevail?

A week later: the limb grows, crooked still

Bang Around

Bang around enough and some-
times something good
comes out. Like, sometimes
even a blind squirrel can find

an acorn. Or not: that's com-
mon, too. So, last night it stormed hard
with thunder rolling around and lightning
lighting up the hills, and our dog, Jessie,

got nervous, came into our bedroom needing
a little re-assurance that things
were OK despite the rattle-bang and
odd lights flashing. The electricity

went off momentarily, I could tell that
because in morning, the electric
clocks on the microwave and the

conventional oven were messed up, lost
in time so I set them, according to NPR time
on the radio, the radio has
battery backup and doesn't get confused

when power goes out for a few
minutes. Now, having said all this and knowing
these words don't carry much
useful meaning, we can

bounce about and play, perhaps, with
some new ideas. Harjo became poet laureate:
she rose
due to good work, and years ago I found

her poems: her lines were very long,
much longer than those
pushed into place by Archie.
And she's a good'un too,
bye.

Way to Go

Achy joints
in the fingers of both hands.
    It's tough
even to type
at first—stiff
tendons and muscles
don't play nice. Let them
warm up.

Got ready by reading
some Ammons: what a
funny guy he was, so self-
absorbed at times and yet so
out-flung too, working hard:
        yes, he succeeded: secured
the virtue of oddity
OK but let's move on
down and in on a swoop or curl or
        flare out
on the skitter-edge of a
widening gyre
yep you got it, looking

for the great
feeling of elation, not its
subset, the corny little kernel called
happy: no
the one we want is
like the Big Kahuna, but not
personified: rather, the sense
of a huge rounded mass of
rarified goodness, extreme

peace and
total understanding.

But here puzzlement, too: wonder
as to the aim of Ezra Pound, how did he
get so tangled up,
lost on a swoop or curl
in more ways than one and
        as a consequence
got cut short: three weeks
in an outdoor steel cage. Clearly
not the way to go

You Know, You Care

1.

One, two, three, four—gotta find a rhythm, a
boisterous buckaroo strong enough to hold
point-guard position and capable of feeding

over and over the ball to the post, pushing
constantly for the clean shot, the bank or the rimless
slip-through sound of ball on net: over

and over, one up, one through. And when the rhythm's
right as rain begin
then, and only then, begin to build in

a hint of where the thing is going: by train
or boat or car, then begin
only then to specify, not a boat: no, it's a tug

2.

rearing its blunt nose from the greasy slop
huge tires hanging on the sides by ropes
lunging
with a roar to do what needs to get done

nuzzling a monster slick-sided ship: or
it's a canoe, almost wakeless, the water-surface
reflecting like glass except
here and there broken

near shore by bulrush, cattails, the soft flat
leaves of long-stemmed lilies, punctuated
periodically by dip of paddle, slow glide.
So what to do when at last you've got it

moving the right way: moving

3.

along at last, beginning at last to slide
the way you want. Well, it is possible to beckon
a reader to test the lines and toss out

the tow-rope, nylon is good, it's
slippery and swells a little, gets strong when wet
though not so durable to weather

compared to polypropylene, but polypropylene
rope is stiff and hard to work with, not much fun.
Change direction

for a moment: dig out *Garbage*, the poem, review it
for structure, feel how it touches
each thing it touches tenderly

4.

then go ahead: rip off
a line or two designed to drill
right into the bone of science—some new

tidbit of knowledge, perhaps, a fragment of
detail: didja know
back in the early Triassic things just

died out from heat, big losses
in species diversity, big reductions in fish
abundance in equatorial regions and

here we are, heading again in that direction,
by gum, doing it, species
beginning now to head north, hurricanes

5.

ramping up in intensity, more opportunities
for violent weather, permafrost
no longer so frosty, it is beginning

to ooze methane, practically all
of the feedback loops are ramping up but all
in the wrong direction. Oh what if

Archie could see us now: he'd stop reading,
put a thumb on *Garbage* (page 70, look it up)
I bet he wouldn't hesitate to opine

and see, just like that you're there, too, cooking
with mustard, reaching out to touch
a reader, reaching out to let them know

you know, you care

I Lost It, Archie

He typed in strips while I wend
words, bending them to fit
the thought or sometimes curling
the thought to fit the words and

occasionally whereas
and amongst the heretofores he broke
outright to something, e.g., outside, that caught
his eye or linked to something

inside that caught a thought un-
attached to some other thought:
Lordy, one could dance
a jig or do the jitterbug just trying to

keep the thing alive: not long
ago (ago), that is, just a short time
in the past, the wife and I were out
in lawn chairs on the deck over-

looking the koi pond and the water was
     yes, splashing and trickling
beautifully down the little water-
fall, and the koi were cruising about

like colorful sub-
marines, looking up
here and there for dinner, whereas
and heretofore we sipped our drinks and they

(the koi) slurped stuff off the water surface while
waiting for their big manna to fall
like usual near dusk amongst the lily pads
and frogs huddled here and there poking

google-eyes up from below the waterline
one can reasonably ask where
is this thing going? Or has it gone
off the rails, irrevocably this time

maybe down a ravine or worse
into a stony river, the bridge
    over which
we ride, chatting sometimes and

singing hallelujah, people
we're passing stand wagging
bright parasols and noshing
popcorn as we

(the inverse of another
roadside attraction)

ride by, a choo-choo chug
feeling to the whole thing, a labored
lurching progress, and I,
yep, still here, still

trying to capture the thing,
like he could and I can't:
more like a hobo, just hanging on, hunched
in a dark corner of a boxcar.

Glisten, Glisten

We are ourselves
pools in a long brook: husked, we
glisten, too, glisten and glisten.

• • •

Say thus to water. Stirring a little
at the head of a pool, you can find

a small group of water-smooth stones,
and finding them there, hesitate, fixed at first,

then curl your fingers around them: the wet-slicked
stones disrupt briefly your motion, disrupt,

for a moment, gravity's steady
draw, its relentless and unremitting

crooked finger calling here,
my lovely, my dear, come this way, it is

slightly lower here than there,
        just

caress that stone on your left and coil
lightly over the other there and around the next —
I'm with you all the way, Bud,
we can do it, together, set things

in motion. Inevitably,
motion: drawn up by the sun,

drawn down by mass
attracting mass, the

interludes and interstices,
apertures, crannies and cracks where

things may slow you, for a moment;
slow, yes, almost to pause. "But

great things await you,"
said father to son: (un-

specified) "Great things."
The path like the things

unspecified;
but even then I knew

each stone is particular
in each aspect, in every dimension—

yet he stepped back, removing
himself so as not to

interfere, he said, with the thread
of great things pending, with things

inevitable as water: things
certain as sun, gravity, stones and life.

• • •

Steps leading up
will not surprise: dreams will

not fog off the higher elevations of
ascension...

... and then all the world cannot fill
the hole which becomes a trillion

miles of nothing

The italicized lines in "Glisten Glisten"— three at the
beginning and seven at end—are from Ammons, A.R. 1997.
Glare (pages 159 and 70, respectively). W. W. Norton &
Company, Inc. New York, NY.

Easter Morning
by A. R. Ammons

 I have a life that did not become,
that turned aside and stopped,
astonished:
I hold it in me like a pregnancy or
as on my lap a child
not to grow old but dwell on

it is to his grave I most
frequently return and return
to ask what is wrong, what was
wrong, to see it all by
the light of a different necessity
but the grave will not heal
and the child,
stirring, must share my grave
with me, an old man having
gotten by on what was left

when I go back to my home country in these
fresh far-away days, its convenient to visit
everybody, aunts and uncles, those who used to say,
look how he's shooting up, and the
trinket aunts who always had a little
something in their pocketbooks, cinnamon bark
or a penny or nickel, and uncles who
were the rumored fathers of cousins
who whispered of them as of great, if
troubled, presences, and school

teachers, just about everybody older
(and some younger) collected in one place
waiting, particularly, but not for
me, mother and father there, too, and others
close, close as burrowing
under skin, all in the graveyard
assembled, done for, the world they
used to wield, have trouble and joy
in, gone

the child in me that could not become
was not ready for others to go,
to go on into change, blessings and
horrors, but stands there by the road
where the mishap occurred, crying out for
help, come and fix this or we
can't get by, but the great ones who
were to return, they could not or did
not hear and went on in a flurry and
now, I say in the graveyard, here
lies the flurry, now it can't come
back with help or helpful asides, now
we all buy the bitter
incompletions, pick up the knots of
horror, silently raving, and go on
crashing into empty ends not
completions, not rondures the fullness
has come into and spent itself from

I stand on the stump
of a child, whether myself
or my little brother who died, and
yell as far as I can, I cannot leave this place, for
for me it is the dearest and the worst,
it is life nearest to life which is
life lost: it is my place where
I must stand and fail,
calling attention with tears
to the branches not lofting
boughs into space, to the barren
air that holds the world that was my world

though the incompletions
(& completions) burn out
standing in the flash high-burn
momentary structure of ash, still it

is a picture-book, letter-perfect
Easter morning: I have been for a
walk: the wind is tranquil: the brook
works without flashing in an abundant
tranquility: the birds are lively with
voice: I saw something I had
never seen before: two great birds,
maybe eagles, blackwinged, whitenecked
and headed, came from the south oaring
the great wings steadily; they went
directly over me, high up, and kept on
due north: but then one bird,
the one behind, veered a little to the
left and the other bird kept on seeming
not to notice for a minute: the first
began to circle as if looking for
something, coasting, resting its wings
on the down side of some of the circles:
the other bird came back and they both
circled, looking perhaps for a draft;
they turned a few more times, possibly
rising—at least, clearly resting—
then flew on falling into distance till
they broke across the local bush and
trees: it was a sight of bountiful
majesty and integrity: the having
patterns and routes, breaking
from them to explore other patterns or
better ways to routes, and then the
return: a dance sacred as the sap in
the trees, permanent in its descriptions
as the ripples round the brooks
ripplestone: fresh as this particular
flood of burn breaking across us now
from the sun.

About the Author

Arthur Stewart's poems have been published in more than a dozen national and regional poetry anthologies and in various literary and scientific magazines, including *Rattle, Journal of the American Medical Association, Lullwater Review, Big Muddy, New Millennium Writings, Bulletin of the Ecological Society of America,* and *Chemical & Engineering News.* He was a 1997 Tennessee Poetry Prize winner, a 2009 winner of the Wilma Dykeman Prize for essay writing, and a 2013 inductee into the East Tennessee Writers' Hall of Fame for poetry. He served as writer-in-residence at Michigan State University's Kellogg Biological Station, and has given science writing workshops for undergraduate, graduate and postgraduate science interns at U.S. Department of Energy facilities in Tennessee, West Virginia, Pennsylvania, South Carolina, Oregon, and Colorado. This chapbook is his eighth published collection of science-inspired poems.

www.ingramcontent.com/pod-product-compliance
Lightning Source LLC
Chambersburg PA
CBHW020443030426
42337CB00014B/1363